THE
Old Photographs
SERIES

BRENTWOOD

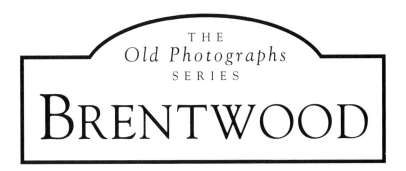

THE
Old Photographs
SERIES

BRENTWOOD

Compiled by
John Copeland & Nick Harris

ALAN SUTTON

BATH • AUGUSTA • RENNES

First published 1994
Copyright © John Copeland & Nick Harris 1994

Alan Sutton Limited
12 Riverside Court
Bath BA2 3DZ

ISBN 07524 0018 5

Typesetting and origination by
Alan Sutton Limited
Printed in Great Britain

Contents

Introduction

Brentwood has been an important stopping place for travellers since Roman times. It was possibly the imperial posting station, Durolitum, and was included as the site for a battle in Robert Graves', *Claudius the God*. Only in the last 150 years have people settled in significant numbers, transforming Brentwood from a hamlet into a major town on the outskirts of the Metropolis.

Cleared from the forest in late Saxon times, Brentwood derived its name from charcoal burners who 'brent' wood to supply the great houses of the neighbourhood. The original hamlet of Brentwood closely equates to the manor of Costed, mentioned in the Domesday Book of 1086 as 459 acres within the parish of South Weald. The manor was granted by William of Wochendone to the Priory of St Osyth and this was confirmed by Henry II in around 1180. The Priory may well have laid out Brentwood as a new settlement as it is first mentioned in 1176.

In 1221, David, the Prior of St Osyth, built the chapel of St Thomas Becket which drew the town's first visitors, pilgrims bound for Canterbury and the magnificent new shrine dedicated to St Thomas. Hubert de Burgh took sanctuary from the King's officers in the chapel in 1223. The market, granted by Henry III in 1277, also attracted a wide range of visitors, many from London. It was held every Wednesday (and later Fridays too) until the end of the eighteenth century in Hart Street, formerly Back Street. In the seventeenth century Brentwood was mentioned as a 'great market town, manufacturing silk rugs of extraordinary beauty'. Peasants rose up from Brentwood in the Revolt of 1381 and centuries later, in 1648, Royalist troops assembled in the town to march on Colchester where they were eventually beseiged by Fairfax.

The most frequent visitors were travellers on the Harwich-London and Ongar-Tilbury routes, and the High Street inns provided 110 beds and stables for 183 horses by 1686. Numbers increased significantly with the advent of the stagecoach – by 1800 four companies were operating the route, especially important for its connection to Harwich and the packet service to Europe. At the height of the service forty stage-coaches stopped each day at the White

Hart. This inn is the only survivor of the nineteen hostelries in the High Street of this period.

In his *Tour thro' the Eastern Counties* (1724) Daniel Defoe noted that Brentwood was a large thoroughfare town, 'full of good inns and chiefly maintained by the excessive multitude of carriers and passengers which are constantly passing this way to London with droves of cattle, provisions and manufactures'.

Whatever its importance as a crossroads, Brentwood remained a small community in the parish of South Weald until the arrival of the Eastern Counties Railway. Authorised in July 1836, the first trains steamed into Brentwood four years later and subsequent developments in the town were centred on the railway.

While half of the land on Brentwood Hall estate on Warley Hill provided the site for the 'Essex Lunatic Asylum' the remainder was sold off in lots for development by the British Land Company. By 1876 Brentwood could be described as 'clean, quiet and well-to-do and rather more "genteel" than is common in Essex towns – the suburbs are pretty and pleasant' (Thorne's *Environs of London*, 1959).

Other arrivals included the military who made camp on Warley Common in 1742 and were visited by both Dr Johnson and George III in 1778. In 1804 the War Office decided to buy land in Great Warley and built barracks there which were finished in 1806. For a time the barracks were occupied by the East India Company but they reverted to the British Army after the Indian Mutiny of 1842. An army presence was maintained in Brentwood until demolition of the barracks began in 1958. Although the Essex Regimental Chapel remains, the site has been used by the Ford Motor Company for offices since 1966. Of the other recent local industries, brewing, brickmaking and Ilford films have all left the town while Thermos still retains an operational factory. A large percentage of the working population now commutes to London and other nearby centres.

The motor car has been the most influential factor in Brentwood's recent history. The town benefitted from the construction of a bypass in the 1960s which now carries more traffic than it was intended to do and will require widening in the near future. The consequences of the construction of the M25, completed in the Brentwood region by the late 1970s, are still being felt.

When Brentwood Urban District Council was set up in 1899 it included 5,000 people and comprised 460 acres on each side of the High Street. By 1993 the newly created borough administered a population of over 70,000.

To celebrate the centenary, this year, of the picture postcard this book is comprised of images taken entirely from postcards of Brentwood and its postal district.

One

Up and Down Memory Lane: the High Street

The William Hunter monument stands at the top of High Street. Erected in 1861, it commemorates the silk-weaver's apprentice who was burnt at the age of 19 on 26th March 1555. His crime was to spurn the doctrine of 'transubstantiation' (the belief that the communion bread and wine is the physical body and blood of Christ). On the left are the original Wilson's stores, constructed around 1889.

These stores were destroyed by a fire that started in a basement paint store on 4th September 1909. The combined efforts of the fire brigade and army from Warley Barracks were unable to prevent complete destruction. Eyewitnesses compared the wax dummies melting in the windows to people screaming for help.

GREAT FIRE AT WILSON AND COY BRENTWOOD

While cracks that the monument suffered were repaired by September 1910, the house adjacent to Wilson's remained in its burnt-out state for nearly forty years until a dispute between the neighbours was resolved and it became part of the stores.

Undeterred by the fire, Wilson's continued to trade in a temporary building until each department was re-established in new premises by 1911. Although the site has been occupied by Cooper's furniture emporium since 1978 the junction is still known as Wilson's corner.

Looking down the High Street in the 1930s, before traffic lights were installed at the corner. One notices several changes from the view in the earlier picture. The outfitter on the right, on which site Woolwich Property Services now stands, had changed hands, street lighting had been introduced and the telegraph poles enlarged. Adjacent to the outfitters was Edes tobacconists and then the Good Intent pub, a recently-renovated homeless shelter.

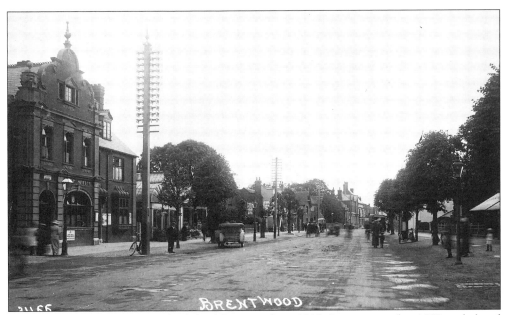

The post office building is on the left of this view from 1912. It was opened in 1892 and closed in 1939.

The modern post office, opened on 21 April 1941, was built on its predecessor's site which was enlarged to include the adjacent Russell's florists.

The Palace cinema in 1929. Opened in 1921, it was managed by Samuel Dorin for 45 years. Although rebuilt in September 1934 to accommodate the 'talkies', such as Broadway, Showboat and Blackmail, it could not compete with television, closing in 1968. Sainsbury's now stands on the site. The Chequer's Inn on the left, which opened in 1769, was replaced by Montague Burton's outfitters in 1937. Only the snooker hall that occupied the first storey has survived.

The Chequers Inn and Lion and Lamb Hotel in 1914. The only remnant of the Lion and Lamb is in the facade of the building now occupied by WHSmith. It was rebuilt in its original Tudor style after it was burnt to the ground in the latter half of the nineteenth century.

The hotel was a less imposing sight by the start of the 1950s as shops sprang up along the High Street. The sign of the Odeon Super cinema, which showed films from 1938 to 1974, can be seen on the left.

The High Street *c*.1913. The awning on the right is that of David Rist, grocer, whose brother also had a grocers shop next to the first building on the left. The Rist family held a large estate at the turn of the century and a Miss Rist owned the last detached house in a garden in the High Street which was only pulled down after the Second World War. Iceland is now on this site.

A similar view from about 1938 lacks the telegraph poles but includes street lighting.

Further down the High street *c.*1910. The shop on the left was an outfitters and haberdashers, J.J. Crowe & Co., later Crowe & Maynard.

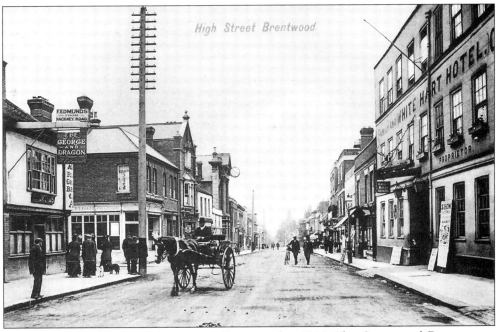

The White Hart hotel and George and Dragon pub *c.*1906. The George and Dragon once played host to the many farmers who brought their wares to the busy Hart street market. The White Hart is one of the oldest buildings in the High Street, named after Richard II who is said to have stayed there in the fifteenth century. Behind the red-brick Georgian facade lies a complex of timber-framed medieval buildings around a coaching yard.

The south end of the High street in about 1917. The Sir Charles Napier, which was once a Methodist chapel, can be seen in the right background. Scott Horne's paper shop can be seen in the right foreground. His stock press on Saturday evenings was for many years the only way to ascertain the day's football and racing results.

The ivy-covered house on the right was the private Academy of Francis Monkhouse which provided for eighty boys between the ages of eight and fifteen, half of whom were boarders. Monkhouse apparently showed his affection for his students by regular beatings and the Academy was closed by 1871 when Monkhouse was listed as an insurance agent. By this time (*c*.1906) the building was in private ownership prior to demolition. Opposite is the house of Dr Mansell, the first doctor in what became the 'Tile House' partnership at the other end of the High Street.

The junction of the High Street with Kings Road *c.*1914. The demolition of the Ind Coope off-licence on the corner and Maynard's haberdasher made way for road widening. On the left is Drakes the Baker whose family, in common with the majority of shopkeepers at the time, lived above the shop.

Looking up the High Street at the turn of the century. The Swan Inn, which was host to William Hunter on the eve of his execution, was rebuilt on this site by 1935. On its left is the residence and solicitor's practice of Brigadier-General Smith, Deputy Lord Lieutenant of Essex. His father, Colonel Smith commanded the Cyprus Battalion in the First World War. H.Wood Fruiterers is on the right.

A view from the late 1940s. The white building in the right foreground is the Bell Inn, which served thirsty customers from 1454 until *c*.1951 and was demolished *c*.1970. Cramphorn's now stands on its site.

We approach the Town Hall, on the right, in the late 1940s. Built in 1864 as a replacement for the Assize House, it was primarily a location for public functions. Demolished in 1963, its site is now occupied by Courts furniture stores.

Compare this view from the early 1920s with the view on page 17. The integrated garage, at this time Clarke's, had smoothly made the transition from dealing with horse-drawn to motor transport.

A comparison of this view from c.1950 with that on page 15 shows the modernisation of the Lion and Lamb Hotel and Unwin's butchers on the left.

The arrow in this view from the end of the nineteenth century shows Arthur Henry Brown, a composer of world-wide renown. He was described by the *Brentwood Gazette* as one of the great pioneers of church music and one of the most remarkable Brentwoodians the town had produced. He died in February 1926, aged 95. Water from the pump in the right foreground was used to settle the road dust.

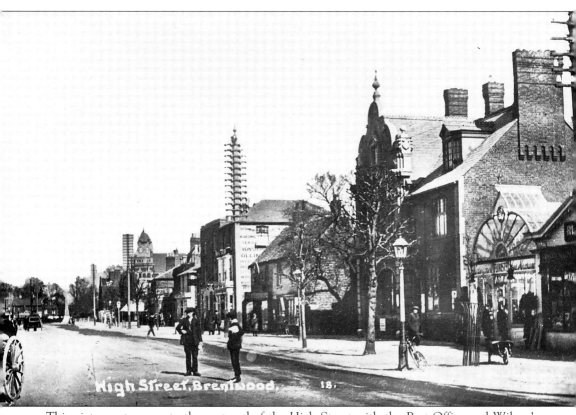

High Street, Brentwood. 18.

This picture returns us to the east end of the High Street with the Post Office and Wilson's stores visible on the right and the Yorkshire Grey on the left. This eighteenth-century pub was closed in 1961 to be replaced by shops.

Two

Highways and Byways

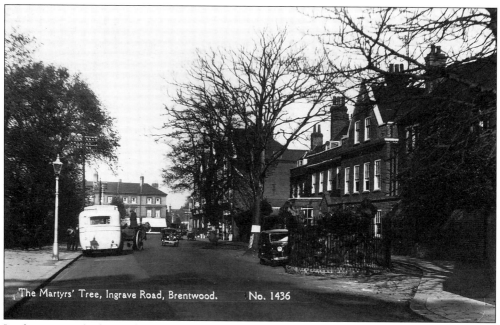

The Martyrs' Tree, Ingrave Road, Brentwood.   No. 1436

Looking towards the High Street on Ingrave Road c.1930. The elm under which the martyr William Hunter is believed to have been burnt is fenced off in the right foreground. It was replaced by an oak in 1936 to commemorate the accession of George IV, and finally removed in 1952.

Corner of Ingrave Road and High Street, Brentwood   No. 457

An earlier photograph of the corner of Ingrave road and the High Street.

St. Thomas' Road in 1906 looking towards Queen's Road

Victorian Crown Street. Across the High Street, the White Hart can be seen. The market was based in this area, behind the Kings Head. The stables of the George and Dragon can be seen adjacent to the lamppost in the right foreground. There was a frequent passage of mounted troops heading to and from Colchester. While the officers were accommodated at the White Hart, the men were billeted around the town. The buildings on the right suffered heavily in the bombing raids of the Second World War which damaged 5,038 buildings and caused 432 casualties.

Queen's Road c.1918. The man on the right may be returning from the station. The nearest house on the left was known as St. Mildreds and housed the telephone exchange for many years. It has now been replaced, although the gateway remains. The spire of the Catholic Cathedral is just visible behind it.

The junction of Queen's Road with King's Road c.1916. On the left is the garden of the Shrubbery, residence of Colonel Fielder and his family, who owned the brewery (see page 31). For a short time this was Russell's Garden Centre, but the site is now occupied by a roundabout.

Cornsland near Rose Valley, a private road before development, *c*.1910.

Rose Valley *c*.1920, seen from just after The Close, looking away from Brentwood. The High School for Girls was at the top of the hill until the mid-1920s when it became a health centre. It has since been pulled down.

King's Road looking over Warley *c.*1900. Two ladies can be seen entering Primrose Hill on the left in front of the Brewery Tap, which formed part of Fielder's brewery. The Baptist church now stands where the wooden photographic studio can be seen on the corner of Chase Road, which has become King's Chase. The open space had been brick fields and was used by travelling entertainments until cottages were erected.

King's Road seen from the junction with Queen's Road, *c.*1917.

Looking across the railway bridge towards Brentwood with Crescent Road running off to the left before the First World War. The sign of the Railway Tavern, run by the Ellis family from 1870 to 1945, can be seen in the left distance.

Crescent Road which was laid out by 1860, showing Sussex Road to the right and a general stores.

The lower part of Warley Hill at the point where Avenue Road branches to the right. The facade of the Methodist church on the right is undergoing modernisation which included the removal of its extravagant pinnacles. It was built in 1892 to replace the chapel in Primrose Hill which was set up by Thomas Wilcox, a Wesleyan navvy from Lincolnshire who was working on the railway extension.

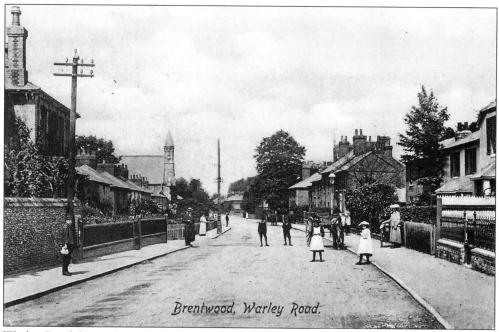

Warley Road from where the Woodman Road joins it and some distance beyond the mental hospital from Brentwood in 1905.

Brook Street Hill, looking rowards London, *c*.1910.

Brook Street looking west at the turn of the century.

Brook Street *c.*1896, before work began on the Homesteads estate. On the left is the Golden Fleece the structure of which is fairly unchanged. Believed to have been built on the site of an earlier priory, parts of the inn can be traced back to the early fifteenth century.

Middleton Hall and Lane *c*.1905. It is also known as Tasker's Lane after Countess Tasker who lived in the hall, now the home of Brentwood Preparatory School.

Honeypot Lane in 1905. While houses have been built at the Brook Street Hill end of the lane, part of its country feel survives lower down. The Weald Road end, however, was rerouted when the by-pass was built.

Park Road *c*.1908. This scene is not very different from the modern view.

Costead Manor Road showing the first major council housing estate, the 'New Hundred' in the mid-1930s. Eight types of two- and three-bedroom houses with all 'mod cons' were offered for a rent of 10s a week.

Ongar Road, seen from the corner near St. George's Church. The track in the foreground was Green Lane and the houses are known as the Scotch Houses because of their individual names.

Ongar Road looking away from Wilson's Corner *c*.1905. The building on the right is the old Rising Sun. The new one was built behind the old, which was pulled down for road widening. A laundry was built on the right where the fencing can be seen. The site is now being developed for housing by Wimpey after an aborted attempt to build offices.

Burland Road, 1903. Only two houses of what is now a substantial development had been built by this time.

Milk delivery on Kimpton Avenue, c.1909, soon after the road was laid out on part of the Robin Hood Meadows which had been owned by the Hill family, who were brewers in Brentwood.

Shenfield Road, early 1920s.

The junction of Shenfield and Ongar Roads with the High Street, late 1920s. Lester House, for many years the home of the Lewis family, became the National and Provincial Bank around 1928, with two shops and chambers above it. It is now a Saffron Walden, Herts and Essex building society. To the right is Old House which has existed since 1748. It has served time as the Red Lion Inn, the Rist family home, part of Brentwood School and London Hospital and then Post Office Telephones before becoming the Arts and Community Centre in 1973. The next was Mrs. Saville's sweet shop until replaced by Eadena House. The steeply-roofed building was the office of Landon's solicitors, rebuilt around 1936 as Landon House. The small traffic island was first replaced by traffic lights and then by two mini-roundabouts.

Three

At Work

Possibly the well-respected and generously-decorated men of the Warley Asylum Fire Brigade
c.1910.

The shopfront of the rebuilt Wilson & Co. c.1920.

A member of the butchers firm, H.Axon making his deliveries in 1910.

A funeral procession presumably from Winter Brothers undertakers in King's Road with the High Street in the background, c.1913.

Hackney Workhouse *c*.1912. Founded as the Agricultural and Industrial school by the London Borough of Shoreditch in 1854, it was the Hackney Union Branch Workhouse and Infants School from 1885 to 1930. St. Faith's Hospital until 1980, it is currently subject to redevelopment.

Fielder's Brewery which produced fine ales from 1863 to 1923. It was taken over by the Hornchurch Brewery.

The South Essex Waterworks company's pumping station at Great Warley in about 1900. The first mains water supply, it relayed water from a reservoir to a water tower on Warley Road near the barracks. Unfortunately the tower could not withstand the pressure and collapsed during its initial filling.

Passengers arriving at the original station from Warley c.1911. Opened in 1840, it was demolished to allow the doubling of the line to Shenfield. A terrace of shops is now on the left where the trees stood.

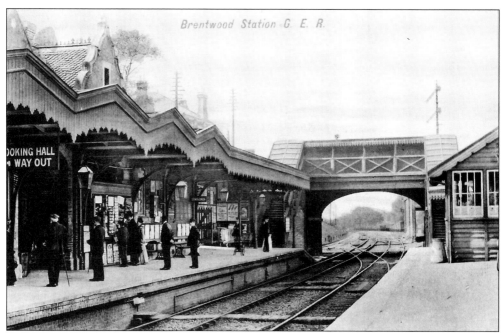

Brentwood Station prior to the duplication of tracks in 1934. Passengers are waiting on the London platform.

The London train passes under the Seven Arches Bridge c.1900. It was built entirely from the bricks of the demolished Mill Green House at Ingatestone. The bridge carries the Hartswood Road over one of the deepest cuttings in the whole eastern system. The 'Tips' at the lower end of Shenfield Common were formed from the excavated material.

48

The Ford headquarters building was built on the site of Warley Barracks and opened in September 1964. The architects were T.P. Bennett and Son.

The Convent of Mercy, founded by Canon John Kyne in 1872. The building has recently been converted into the offices of the Roman Catholic Bishop of Brentwood.

Highwood Hospital *c.*1925

A group of children and nurses at the hospital *c.*1908

Brentwood Convalescent Home for Children, 55, Weald Road, which was founded in 1889.

The original Brentwood District Hospital at the edge of Shenfield Common. Known as the cottage hospital, the original cottage shown was rebuilt in 1895 by Dr Quennell. Additions were made before 1930 when its capacity was reached and it was decided to erect a new building. For a time a maternity home, it has now become part of the Four Oaks flats.

The present Brentwood District Hospital built on land donated by Percy Bayman. £40,000 was raised by public subscription, the foundation stone was laid in May 1933 by Princess Mary and it was opened on June 14th 1934 by Princess Helena Victoria.

The front of the County Asylum, Warley c.1905, now the Warley hospital main building. Built primarily on the Brentwood Hall estate, the Kavanagh family seat, the first sections were ready for occupation in 1853.

Four
Freetime

Brentwood Carnival 1909. The procession through town ended on Shenfield Common.

The Common in quieter times *c*.1905. In the 1840s the land north of the railway line was deemed to be 'common' but it was not regulated until an Act of Parliament in 1881, under the recommendation of which a committee of conservators was set up in 1884. In July 1900 an order was made to prosecute people who took water from the ponds.

Looking south across the common the spire of St. Thomas' church, finished in 1886, can be seen in the background. The bandstand stood in an acoustic hollow created by the removal of gravel from the common and was used regularly until the end of the century. It was demolished by 1913 but in very dry weather, such as the summer of 1976, its site can still be seen in the grass.

The common c.1911. The avenue of limes were planted in 1895 by students and unemployed men. £60 was provided for the activity by the great Brentwood philanthropist and author, John Larkin.

The mill pond derives its name from the two windmills which used its water. Part of Ye Olde Logge was a smithy at this time (c. 1910) and carts went in the pond to swell the wood on the wheels after the fixing of iron tyres. Two ponds were joined to create the present pool and there used to be at least three additional ponds in which all varieties of native newts were to be found.

Children have always enjoyed the mill pond. Fishing at the turn of the century.

Less sedate pursuits in 1950.

For a time there was a sand pit in the common.

The open-air swimming pool was built in Debtor's Fields, North Road, behind the High Street, at a cost of £8,000. Opened on August Bank Holiday 1935 it was an immediate success (1,000 people paid merely to watch over the first week-end) and remained popular until its closure in 1980, to be replaced by the Hambro computer centre.

The County Asylum Coronation Cricket Team in 1908.

The Feast of the Sacred Heart, 1912, was organised by the Catholic Church in addition to processions to Our Lady Corpus Christi and other events.

Brentwood Parish Church from St. Thomas' Road *c*.1910.

The ruins of the chapel of St. Thomas à Becket soon after they had been conserved and railed off in 1902. It was founded in 1221 by David, Abbot of St. Osyth. The ruins serve as a memorial of the actions of thirty spinsters, led by Thomasine Tyler, on 5 August 1577. They staged a 'Tudor sit-in' to prevent the workmen of Wistan Browne, nephew and heir of Sir Anthony, from pulling it down. The chapel was the home of the National Boys School from 1836 to 1867. On the right is the Priory which made way for the Odeon cinema and is now the site of the Chapel High shopping centre.

The Parade Cinema c.1920 was very popular until its closure in 1940. This and the other buildings shown, which include Barrett's coal merchants, Smith's hardware and the Auction House, have provided the site for a row of offices

The Foresters Inn, which now forms part of Ye Olde Logge.

The Seven Arches Tavern on the Harts Wood side of the railway line, *c.*1903.

Five

Schooldays

Brentwood School seen from the Ingrave Road, showing the main school buildings which were opened on 25th June 1910.

The old part of the school, built in 1568 and of which only the outer walls and a doorway remain, with the chapel on the right and the martyr's tree in front.

This aerial shot from 1925 shows the completed Memorial Hall between the wings of the 1910 building and work to extend the school chapel (top middle of the picture). It was founded as a grammar school for any boy from the parishes within a three mile radius who could read and write, in 1558. Its benefactor was the parish Squire and Chief Justice on Common Pleas, Sir Anthony Browne who was supposedly prompted by regret at his involvement with the execution of William Hunter three years earlier. The school now has over a thousand pupils of whom a quarter are boarders. Conditions have changed since the rules were legally redrawn in 1622 when the boys were expected to attend from six until six in the summer.

St. Helen's School. It was opened in 1861 in what was built as St. Helen's Church in 1837.

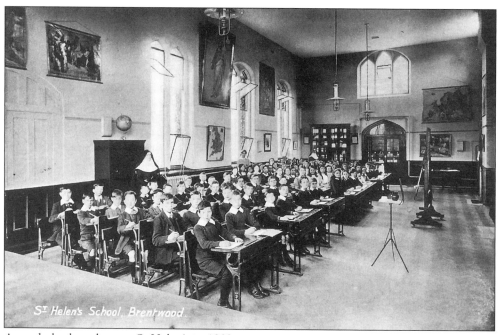

An orderly class photo at St Helen's in 1903.

Going for a walk, Ursuline Convent, Brentwood, Essex.

A view of the west side of Ursuline Convent which was founded on 23rd April 1900. The Ursuline Order, from Forest Gate, originally opened the school in Matlock in Queen's Road before it moved to its present location at the junction of Queen's and Earlsfield Roads. Originally totally independent it is now a voluntary-aided school.

The Children, Ursuline Convent, Brentwood, Essex.

The small convent attracted pupils and teachers from near and far. This postcard was sent by a sister at the convent to her mother in Paris.

The typing room, Ursuline Convent, after the Second World War.

The senior class photo *c.*1926.

The senior string ensemble at the convent from the same year.

The expansion of the County School for Girls forced the move to this site from Montpelier House, at the corner of Rose Valley and Queen's Road in 1927. The school was founded by Kate Bryan in 1876 as a private school but was taken over by the county council after the First World War.

St. Charles' Roman Catholic Schools, Weald lane. The St. Charles' treatment centre, built on its site, was opened in 1971 for children aged between twelve and eighteen.

St Charles' Schools were managed by the Brothers of Mercy until 1900, the Sisters of Charity until 1936 and the Irish Christian Brothers until their closure in 1954.

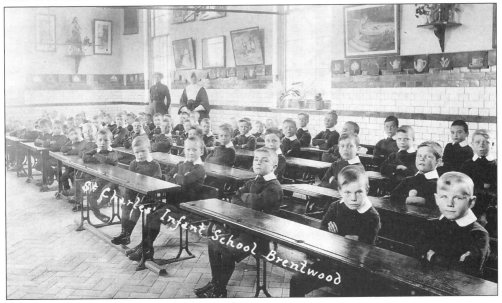

The well-trained infants at St Charles' in 1911.

Highwood Schools for girls and boys with tuberculosis. Charles Downing, who is in the centre of the picture, helped with the building of the schools and worked in the grounds for many years. The buildings have been used to care for a variety of patients, most recently as Little High Wood Mental Hospital which closed in the late 1970s.

Six

For King and Country

Warley Barracks before the First World War. Most of the buildings have been demolished but its memory survives in some of the road names. Eagle Way is called after the standard of the 44th Foot Regiment captured from the 62nd French Regiment on July 22 1812. The artefacts that were housed at the Eagle Way Museum were moved to the Chelmsford and Essex Museum in the early 1970s.

The married quarters, Warley Barracks.

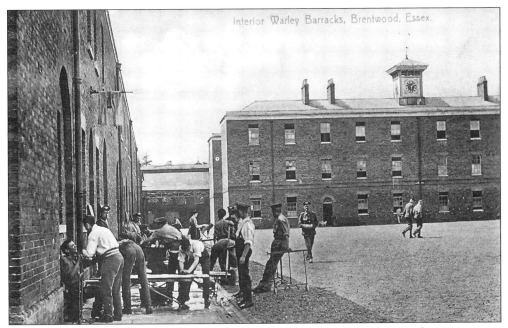

The barracks interior, where the 3rd East Anglian Regiment was brought into shape.

A military funeral en route to the cemetery at Lorne Road from Warley Barracks.

The Queen's Regiment arrives at Brentwood station, February 21 1910. Their uniform included sun hats suited to the African climate from which they were returning.

The regiment's arrival at the barracks.

Parade in the quadrangle, Warley Barracks.

General French inspects WAACs at Warley, 1917.

The Second Battalion Middlesex Regiment bayonet fighting team, winners of the regimental tournament 1911/12/13, photographed by Thornton Cousins.

Members of the Regiment's performing society *c*.1913.

A balloon prepares for take off in 1910 from the area on which the barracks gymnasium, now Keys Hall, was built.

The 1st Norfolk Regiment leaving Brentwood, 1909.

This drill hall in Ongar Road had a stage and was used for entertainments and badminton. Later it was a storage building for Eade's the tobacconists and then was converted to become part of the shops known as Hunter's walk. It was finally demolished for the construction of the North Service Road.

The Prince of Wales, later Edward VIII, having left Warley Barracks with the grenadier guards in 1914, passes Warley hospital en route to Wellington Barracks.

A First World War battalion at the barracks.

A similar group in the Second World War.

I am thinking of you at Brentwood

The lonely lot of a soldier garrisoned at Brentwood.

Seven

South Weald, Warley and Great Warley

A view of South Weald church from Wigley Bush Lane from the 1930s of which little has changed. Until the end of the nineteenth century South Weald was the mother parish of Brentwood and the Domesday book, completed by 1086, notes 100 inhabitants.

Leaving St. Peter's church after afternoon service c.1910. Early twelfth century in origin, the tower was built in 1500 and the body of the church was restored by the Reverend Charles Belli in 1868 to the design of S.S. Teulon, who was also responsible for the nearby almshouses and National School buildings. It is popular with brass-rubbing enthusiasts as the oldest brasses date back to 1480.

The old cottages beside the church *c.*1904

The front view of the Rochetts facing the lake. Built in 1770 it was set in a thousand acres. Until 1823 it was the residence of John Jervis, an admiral in Nelson's navy who adopted the title Earl St. Vincent, which is now used as the name of a tiny hamlet not far from Rochetts farm. Octavius Coope MP, partner in the Romford brewery, Ind Coope, lived there from 1863 to 1886. After it was partially destroyed by fire in 1975 planning permission was given to use the building as a training school for hotel staff.

How Hatch. It was built at the turn of the nineteenth century in stock brick and was later extended in red brick.

Weald Hall, 1904. A building had stood on the site since 1062 which was reputedly connected to the St. Thomas chapel by a tunnel. Mary Tudor was reputedly born there and Queen Elizabeth I visited when it was the home of Anthony Browne. The 428 acre site which is now Weald Country Park was also the home of the Tower family before the hall was demolished in 1951.

Weald Road between Brentwood and South Weald.

Weald Road c.1908. The building on the left of the picture is St. Charles' school (see pages 72-3).

An early advertisement for the Tower Arms Hotel, 1913, earlier called the Spread Eagle or Eagle and Crown. A fine example of early eighteenth-century architecture, the date 1704 and initials ALLA are inscribed above the entrance.

The Weald Almshouses before 1914 in the left foreground. The chapel was founded by Sir Anthony Browne concurrently with Brentwood School and rebuilt in the nineteenth century to a design by S.S. Teulon.

Two ladies respectfully dismount before passing Queen Mary's Chapel around 1900. It derives its name from Mary Tudor, who is supposed to have used the small residence as a chapel.

The Avenue, Warley c.1910. This postcard was sent in September 1914 and the writer notes 'we saw train-loads of soldiers go through Brentwood station the other day. I expect they were going to Harwich. We heard the blackberries had been poisoned by German spies at South Weald but of course it is only a rumour.'

Headley Common, showing the Headley Arms c.1916. Taking its name from Lord Headley of the Allanson-Winn family, a former lord of the manor, the title is held today by Charles Rowland. It was well patronised by soldiers from Warley Barracks until the barracks' closure but was rebuilt to become a bar and restaurant.

Christ Church School around the turn of the century. Educating five- to fourteen-year-old children it was described by F.G.Hall as 'late nineteenth-century Essex County Councilesque'.

Great Warley Street approaching the village and the Thatcher's Arms with the road to Brentwood on its right.

Great Warley village, with the Thatcher's arms on the right and The Green and medieval house, Wallets, on the left. The road leading to Tyler's common can be seen on the left as little more than a track.

A child waits patiently for his or her father outside the Thatcher's Arms. In stark comparison with the Headley Arms this pub has changed little since this 1920s picture. While in the previous two pictures beer from the local Hornchurch Brewery was served, the Thatcher's was owned by Mann, Crossman and Paulin after 3rd December 1925.

The village post office at Great Warley. The cottages looking onto the Green range in origin from the fifteenth to eighteenth centuries.

The marriage of Miss Muriel Heseltine to General de Rougemont, the Goldings, 28th May 1914. In the background is the church of St Mary the Virgin, which was designed by Charles Harrison Townsend and Sir William Reynolds Stephens between 1902 and 1904. The cost, £5,000, was covered by Evelyn Heseltine, who owned the Goldings estate, in memory of his brother Arnold who had died in 1897. The spacious gardens at the Goldings were open to the public in the Summer and the property is now the New World Hotel.

Golding's cottages and Tooks Farm, with Mr Butts, the cutler, who in addition to sharpening knives performed all manner of other repairs.

A master outside Great Warley school.

Eight
Hutton and Shenfield

Hutton Village and the Chequers Inn in 1905.

Brickley Estate, Hutton in the 1950s. Built on land that was originally the farm of Hutton Poplars (see page 99), it later became the London County Council Estate.

The boy's side of Hutton Industrial School, one of several such establishments in the area. Built by the Poplar Board of Governors in 1906 at a cost of £160,000, it replaced an orphanage in Stratford that was destroyed by fire. The leading figure behind the poplars was the famous MP, George Lansbury.

The girl's side of the school.

Sunray Parade *c*.1935.

Hutton wash - the perfect spot for a paddle.

The top of Hutton village *c*.1912.

A view of the bottom end at about the same time.

Hutton High Road about 1908 by the cottages looking towards Shenfield.

The High Road in 1940.

Church Lane, Hutton, between the wars.

Hutton Mount 1905, which has maintained much of the character of this view.

Shenfield Post Office and the Green Dragon *c.*1905. Established in 1893 by William Tabor, the postmistress at this time was Mrs. Harriet Tabor, who was in charge from 1899 to 1914.

The Eagle and Child Inn *c.*1912 – the eagle was unavailable for this photograph!

Priest's Lane *c.*1914. This card is dated 17th January 1917 and X marks the spot where the only bomb to be dropped on Shenfield in the First World War landed. It killed Nurse Evans who was on leave from France and all the windows as far as the tree were smashed while dirt was thrown up onto the roofs. The houses were built at the turn of the century, the beginning of the development of Glanthams Farm Estate.

Shenfield and Hutton Station and booking hall on the Great Eastern Railway in 1923 when the station was built at the junction of the Southend and Norwich Lines. On the right of the picture is the old station-master's house, then occupied by Mr. Meehan. Next door is the tiny booking office. The only shop in the area was next to the station and owned by Miss Cruise.

By 1935 there was a new Shenfield Station serving trains on the London and North East railway. Note the bridge had also been strengthened and widened.

Railway cottages with the Junction pub on the right from the Hutton side of the station.

Hoping to catch the last train to London? A ladies cross country race in 1924.

The Lych Gate at St. Mary the Virgin Church, Shenfield. The name of the village may derive from Chenefield, meaning field of oaks. It is thus fitting that much of the attraction of this seven-hundred-year-old building should come from its use of this wood. The tower of the National School, built in 1893, can be seen to the left.

St. Mary's Primary School c.1908. Founded in the 1860s, the tower was built in 1893 and dedicated to the Reverend Thomas. It was extended in 1937 and an infants' school was added in 1954.

Nine
Villages to the North

The Post Office, Navestock Side, which no longer exists.

Navestock Church.

The Black Horse, Pilgrim's Hatch. Recorded as a pub and bakery in 1621, it sold bread to Canterbury-bound pilgrims.

Thoby Priory c.1915. Founded in the twelfth century, it was named after the first Prior, Tobias or Toby. Wolsey appropriated it in order to endow colleges. It was then demolished and rebuilt as a private house, incorporating some of the original fabric. There was a serious fire in 1893 and it was again rebuilt. In 1920 it was bought by the Earl of Arran, famous as a newspaper columnist, but was demolished in 1955. Two of its arches remain in what is now a scrap-yard.

Mountnessing, named after the Mountney family, who were lords of the manor, from Church Road c.1905. The pond is now a small garden. Five old cottages depended on this well. A fine example of an early nineteenth-century post-mill, the windmill is believed to have been built in 1807 and was worked by four successive generations of the Agnis family between 1817 and 1937. It was restored to working order in 1983 by Essex County Council and the Friends of Mountnessing Windmill.

The middle building of this view is the mixed school which has remained unchanged apart from the loss of the clock hands and roof turrets. The furthest structure is the Parish Room.

The Post Office, Kelvedon Common. The location of this office has changed fairly regularly.

St. Nicholas Church, Kelvedon Common c.1910. Consecrated on All Saints Day, 1 November 1895 by the Lord Bishop of Colchester, the exterior is virtually unchanged today except for a wooden fence which replaced the hedge.

The crossroads at Kelvedon Hatch, which was owned by Westminster Abbey, showing the church in the background.

Looking up the main road towards the village c.1917. In front of the single storey mill cottage, Mill Lane leads from School Road. The gate in the foreground is of Mushroom Hall. On the cap of the smock windmill is a six-bladed fantail which was taken from the demolished Bentley mill in 1915. It is a more efficient means of turning the mill to the prevailing wind than the wheel and chain method. The Kelvedon Common mill was demolished in 1920.

Kelvedon Common stocks, 1905.

The Whipping Post, Stondon, before the First Word War, a relic of the harsher side of nineteenth-century village life.

Dudbrook, 1908.

Ten

Scenes from the South

Herongate c.1907. The Green Man is on the right.

The Green Man in Herongate in the mid-1920s.

The building in the middle on the left is the Post Office. The Postmistress from 1926 to 1933 was Mrs. Emma Maud King, the publisher of this card, who can be seen with her son, standing by the wall.

The road to East Horndon c.1923. The Boar's Head can be seen in the distance.

Herongate Common in the 1920s.

The rear of Boar's Head and the pond in the 1920s.

The front of Boar's Head c.1920.

Blacksmiths Row, East Horndon *c*.1911

East Horndon rectory.

The Railway Hotel, East Horndon.

Thorndon Hall, which was converted into eighty-five one- to four-bedroom flats in the early 1980s by Thomas Bates and Son Ltd., looking over the golf course. Built between 1764 and 1770 it was designed by James Paine and landscaped by Capability Brown. The visit of George III in 1778 to the home of Robert Edward, 9th Lord Petre was momentous as he was the first monarch to stay in a catholic household since the reformation.

The Petre Chapel in Thorndon Park, West Horndon.

Thorndon Lodge, Ingrave.

The cricket green, Ingrave.

Ingrave Rectory, seen here in 1909, was built in 1890.